The Horsemen of the
Apocalypse in Latin America

The Horsemen of the Apocalypse in Latin America

By Gualdo Hidalgo

The Horsemen of the Apocalypse in Latin America.
© Gualdo Hidalgo, 2015.

Of this edition:

Latin News Agency.

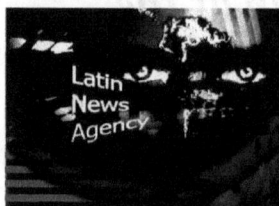

For information, write:
Latin News Agency
ISBN-13: 978-0692467428
ISBN-10: 0692467424
BISAC: Political Science / Commentary & Opinion

Executiveeditor@latinnewsagency.us

A Latin News Agency Edition.

The Horsemen of the Apocalypse in Latin America

By Gualdo Hidalgo

| Latin News Agency, New York

In the beginning there was chaos, personified in the transmutation of Lenin in the essential deity of Marxism during the conflagration of the Russian Revolution of 1917.

The Kingdom of Heaven proclaimed by the Son of God, and the ancillary dream of Paradise restored after the expulsion promulgated by God was replaced by a reign of terror, offered to the Russian people by the sweetener propaganda of the Bolshevik Party as the ultimate realization of paradise on Earth.

Frantically crossing the Russian tundra, with the excruciating crunch of hooves cracking the bones and flesh of its victims, the Beast of the Apocalypse arrives triumphantly in Havana in January, 1959.

In apotheosis of cheers and clamor of revolutionary slogans, whose deafening echoes resound in streets and squares, an unwary people celebrate the beginning of their extermination, persecution and imprisonment.

Deprived of the right to visit other countries -in a sad imitation of the Russians-, Cubans began a harrowing journey of more than half a century to the outrage, meanness, hunger and degradation: to the firing squads, prisons and interrogation cells of the State Security and police station.

The specter of communism began touring Latin America.

With defiant and runaway trot, the Riders of Apocalypse in Latin America – Castro, Maduro, Ortega, Evo Morales and Correa-, with the impetus of an irrepressible devotion, are engaged in the "apostolic mission" of converting the countries of the region to the terrifying communist dictatorship of Cuba, assuming and multiplying themselves in the unholy trinity: as demons, antichrists and false prophets.

As demons claim for themselves the deep obeisance due to the socialist gods; as antichrists, they supplant the Son of God and pretend to be the new Redeemers; and as false prophets claim to be the incarnation of the sacrosanct and savior spirit of Marxism.

This trinity has managed to extend their control and power in Latin America by lies, fraud, deception and trickery.

Marxism and Nazism are the two apocalyptic doctrines of the twentieth century.

Like Lenin in 1917 and Castro in 1959, Hitler destroyed the democracy system of the Weimar Republic, replacing the Third Reich, depriving the Germans of the most basic civil and constitutional rights and assuming absolute power in Germany: Reich President (head of state), Reich Chancellor (head of government), and Fuehrer (head of the Nazi party).

These three representatives of Revelation (Lenin, Hitler and Castro) are the symbol of a despotic power governed by the principle "The Homeland is me."

Driven by the belief that their regimes were the upper and final stage of history and that they would rule infinitely in time, Communists and Nazis were engaged in the fierce suppression of the "representatives of evil": For communists, capitalists; for Nazis, the Jews. To justify and make more palatable their erratic policies they resorted to the use and distortion of the past. Castro did it in the crudest imaginable way by expressing about the heroic mambises: "Today, they had been like us. We, yesterday, had been like them". And to José Martí –who passed away almost seventy years before Castro's guerrilla warfare, he made him an accomplice of the 26 Movement, and one of the attackers of Moncada, in 1953: "He also participated", Castro stated.

Ironically, Hitler justified his monstrous crimes-including the Holocaust -citing the tradition of the Christian faith of the German people. In the book "On the Jews and Their Lies" written by the eminent German theologian Martin Luther, who died four centuries before Nazism, Luther calls Jews "poisonous worms" -a term which brings to mind the "worms" of Castro and the "bugs" of Lenin, and urges to expel them from Germany or condemn them to forced labor, burn their prayer books, their homes, their synagogues, their schools, take their money and their property away; and what cannot be destroyed by fire, cover it with trash so that absolutely no one can ever see again stone or ashes of Jews.

Taking advantage of the secular anti-Semitic tradition, Hitler ordered the pogroms of The Night of Broken Glass in which dozens of Jews were killed and about 30 000 were taken to concentration camps; houses, synagogues, schools and hospitals of the Jews were destroyed. The streets of Germany woke up covered with broken windows of the houses, shops and other Jewish buildings.

Similarly, the Castro regime has been characterized by its atrocities: executions and arbitrary arrests without judicial process or lacking the minimum procedural guarantees; physical and mental torture; layoffs and persecution for religious and political reasons; threats, coercion and blackmail of all kinds.

The rigor of Castro's repression has gone beyond the limits of foolishness and absurdity; like sentencing for illegal attempt to leave the country a drunk stuck at sea riding his horse; or the guy who tried a sandwich on a cafe and said that it tasted bad and was sanctioned by enemy propaganda: the snack was "a product of the Revolution"; or the one who told her indiscreet wife that overnight he had dreamed about people running in the Plaza of the Revolution, and he was convicted of plans to assassinate the Commander in Chief (Fidel Castro).

The brutal suppression of innocent people, the mass imprisonment, repression, assaults and beatings -as currently carried out in Cuba against the Ladies in White and other dissidents- demonstrate the baseness and criminal essence of communist messianism and its dictatorial regimes.

Both Marxism and Nazism apocalyptic doctrines share the "scientific" character but in practice are externalized in a gloomy Hitler measuring human skulls with pinpoint accuracy to prove the superiority of the Aryan, and the ridiculous idiocy of Fidel Castro's intensive growth of moringa –a wild tree with no use for Cubans- to feed people and support the crumbling Cuban economy.

Interestingly, Karl Marx, an avowed atheist, to the extent expressed in "A Contribution to the Critique of Hegel's Philosophy of Right" that "religion is the opium of the people", builds his vision of history against the background of Judaism, the Roman Catholic Church and under the influence, perhaps unconscious, of biblical texts.

The division of history into four major periods, the last of which is capitalism, after which supposedly begins the magnificent golden age of communism, is a Marxist version of the exegesis of the Catholic Church.

Marx does not escape the influence of Hegel and the German tradition of dividing history into four main phases, established by Thomas Muenzter, inspired by the Book of Daniel. Consequently, the Marxist theory of history is an extrapolation based on the Jewish apocalyptic tradition.

The essential difference of Marxism with the prevailing beliefs in medieval times, when apocalyptic fantasies and the awaiting for the Final Judgment of God proliferated –fulfilled on Earth with the return of Christ, and after which, transcending history and time, all will occur in the celestial sphere, in Paradise or Hell- for the Communists, the Last Judgment takes place on Earth, under the iron dictatorship of the proletariat, with arrests and mass executions in summary trials, with the First Secretary of the Party transformed into the revered God.

During the implementation of the earthly communist paradise, they proceed to the identification of "bad and good", a purifying work that in Cuba is entrusted to the Committee for the Defense of the Revolution (CDR), the police and State Security. An aberrant bunch of informers and snitches, hoes, unconditional, careerists, liars, torturers and criminals are exalted to the upper range of the chosen, the "revolutionaries" -"the highest level that the human species can reach", according to Che Guevara.

The Horsemen in Latin America -Castro, Maduro, Ortega, Correa, and Evo Morales- yearn to enthrone in all countries of the region the model of the Cuban

Revolution -the fable of a successful revolution that a cunning Fidel Castro has smuggled for them.

Castro, the revolutionary who never existed, has been in reality throughout his entire life, a dealer of lies, nonsenses, and chimeras. For the successful completion of his trading in lies, he has taken advantage of the absolute isolation and inaccessibility in which he keeps the medieval village called Cuba.

It is urgent that fans of the "heroic" socialist revolution of Castro, defiant of the Empire, awaken from their pernicious lethargy. In fact, the Castro regime has been unmasked of its bygone alleged heroism to become a mendicant Revolution that implores the crumbs of United States, and survives with dollars of the lucky "worms" who managed to escape from the communist Hell of the island, which is deceptively advocated as Paradise on Earth by the Riders of Latin American Apocalypse.

Explanatory note:

In order not to assume an irreverent attitude, and without evidences to contradict the Venezuelan authorities, I have refrained from including the extinct commander Hugo Chavez among the Horsemen of the Apocalypse in Latin America.

Senator Miguel Abdon Saguier, the president of the Authentic Radical Liberal Party (PLRA) of Paraguay, has described the leftist regime of Venezuela as a "spiritualist socialism, esoteric socialism that invokes the spirits and the birds appear," referring to repeated official and public testimony of Nicolas Maduro about his encounters with Hugo Chavez reincarnated as Pajarito (A little bird).

The president reported the appearance of a bird for the first time last April 2, at the start of the electoral campaign for the elections of April 14, when on a visit to the southwestern state of Barinas, reported that he found a "bird chiquitico" with whom he shared whistles and it reminded him to Chavez: "I felt the spirit of Chavez and felt it there like giving us a blessing, and telling us: "The campaign starts today; Go to victory", he said at that time.

On another occasion, President Nicolas Maduro said that the late President Hugo appeared again as a bird after the first appearance in April: "Look, look ... The bird is looking for me. Look, it passed through here. Then people say I am making up things... And he passed singing. That bird is happy because I'm working", Maduro said during a ceremony in the southwestern state of Merida.

About the Author

Gualdo Hidalgo by the Hudson River, West New York, New Jersey, 1996.

Gualdo Hidalgo was born in Bayamo, Cuba, in August, 1951.

When he was 7 years old, he fled with his father, who was in danger of being killed because he used to travel for business to the area where Fidel Castro's guerrilla opera-ted.

Living at the guerrilla whereabouts as a child, he met Fidel Castro, Raul Castro, and he spent two months at Che Guevara's guerrilla headquarter located in El Hombrito, Cuba, while his father stayed there for business with the peasants.

When the author was 11 years old, he delivered a speech -aired live by Cuban TV and Radio Havana Cuba during an event celebrating an anniversary of guerrilla Third Front led by Commander Juan Almeida.

He started his teaching career in 1975 as Chief of the Department of Philosophy at a Cuban military academy. Later he worked as Head of the Department of Political Studies at the Provincial Institute of Labor Studies, Cuba. He also lectured on Philosophy and Economics at the National School of Economy Administration, Cuba.

Furthermore, he graduated from the National School of Broadcasting and The Cuban National Institute of Radio and TV, Havana, Cuba as broadcaster and screenwriter. He is one of the founders of the TV Channel Tele Cristal, Holguin, Cuba.

Gualdo Hidalgo has taught Philosophy, Economics, Spanish Language and Literature, Culture, Politics and TESOL for colleges and universities. He is also a Spanish/English translator and has translated for many corporate institutions, such as Colgate Palmolive, Chase Manhattan Bank, New York City Department of Transportation, etc. Also, he graduated from Shenandoah University, Winchester, Virginia, United States, as a teacher of English as a Second Language. Currently, He holds two outstanding teaching licenses from United States Department of Education.

He immigrated to the US in 1990 as a former Cuban political prisoner.

Hidalgo has been profiled on books published in London and New York by Georgetown University, Harvard University and Freedom House. On the Program Report on Human Rights, 2010, Columbia University requested from Hidalgo to comment about the quality of Columbia University Human Rights Programs.

Gualdo Hidalgo has been declared by the Republic of Argentina, by Decree 730 of the Minister of Innovation and Culture, as a Person of International Cultural Importance.